MW01153131

From the Farm to the Table

Potatoes

by

Kathy Coatney

Copyright @ 2013, 2014 by Kathy Coatney

www.kathycoatney.com

From the Farm to the Table Series
From the Farm to the Table: Potatoes
Book 4

All rights reserved

No part of this publication can be reproduced or transmitted in any form or by any means, electronic or mechanical, without permission in writing from Kathy Coatney

CONTENTS

Reviews from Adults

This book is a perfect segue for introducing primary grade school children to difficult matematical concepts such as acre, mile, pound, ton and century. Age-appropriate vocabulary words are listed and found in bold in the text. Second and third graders study of their community, farming and outdoor jobs including agriculture would find this book entertaining, as well as educational.

   –Rachel Curran, retired elementary teacher administrator

From the Farm to the Table series is absolutely amazing. It has provided our students with a field trip in a book. As they read the books or the book is read to them they become aware of facts and information at their level which has caused them to want to learn more. It is also especially great that they have a list of sight words that can be used with our English language arts curriculum.

   –James Hall, after school program coordinator

Kathy Coatney's From the Farm to the Tablel series brings agriculture to life. These books provide information on farm life and agriculture in an interesting and informative way. Each book provides a list of key vocabulary words that can be used in the classroom setting. Kathy's photos are amazing and provide a concrete way for the reader to experience and understand agriculture. I look forward to seeing what comes next.

   –Patti Thurman, assistant superintendant educational
   services

What Kids are saying about From the Farm to the Table books

I like the bee book. The Queen bee parts are awesome.
I love honey. It's so sweet and yummy. They're really cool pictures. I didn't know what the bee looked like until I read the book.

Emma, age 9

Lots of cool facts. The bees sort of scared me (I don't like bees). The bee book was cool. So was the cow book. I liked both books.

J.J., age 11

Dedication

Thanks to Farmer Terry for his time and entertaining stories. A special thanks to Connor and Peyton for sharing their French fries with me.

Acknowledgements

Many thanks to those who have assisted me with this project. Georgia Bockoven, who put the idea in my head. Patti Thurman, and Jenny Reilly, who consulted and proofread for me. To my email check-in pals, Jennifer Skullestad and Lisa Sorensen, a huge thanks. Luann Erickson, Susan Crosby, Karol Black, and Tammy Lambeth, who critiqued and supported me through the process. To the Redding Lunch Bunch, Libby, Shari, Dianna, Lisa, Terry, and Patti, you're the best. To my family, Nick, Wade and Devin, Collin and Ellis, Jake and Emily, Allie and Russell. You all have been my inspiration. Thank you. I never would have made it without you.

Note to parents and teachers: The words underlined are second-grade vocabulary words. A list of the words used can be found at the end of the book.

Also By

Thank you for reading **From the Farm to the Table** Potatoes, book 4 in **From the Farm to the Table series** of picture books.

I love hearing from my fans. You can contact me through my website: www.kathycoatney.com.

From the Farm to the Table

From the Farm to the Table Dairy
From the Farm to the Table Bees
From the Farm to the Table Olives
From the Farm to the Table Potatoes
From the Farm to the Table Almonds
From the Farm to the Table Beef

Stand Alone Picture Book
Dad's Girls

From the Farm to the Table Potatoes

Farmer Terry holding Russet Norkotah potatoes

Farmer Terry is a spud guy. Spuds or taters are potatoes, and he grows 300 acres of spuds.

Farmer Terry loves farming. His two favorite things about farming are being his own boss and working outside where he is <u>surrounded</u> by wildlife and fresh air.

Seedling potatoes about to be planted

Farmer Terry worked all through high school changing sprinkler pipes for other farmers. In high school, he and his older brother, John, planted and raised 20 acres of potatoes.

Farmer Terry driving a tractor

In college, Farmer Terry drove a big tractor that pulled a potato bulker that is also called a digger and dug potatoes for other farmers.

Russet Norkotah potato

Today, Farmer Terry raises two kinds of potatoes. The first is a variety called Russet Norkotah, which is a big brown potato. The second kind is a variety called a Red potato, that is round and red.

Russet potatoes being harvested for the fresh
market

Farmer Terry's Russet potatoes are
sold into the fresh market. The fresh
market is for a potato that isn't
processed. It is sold raw, uncooked, in
the produce section of the grocery
store.

Farmer Terry holds a newly planted Red potato

Farmer Terry's Red potatoes are sold to a processor who makes them into potato salad that you can buy ready to eat.

Peyton, Farmer Terry's granddaughter, eating French fries

Potatoes can be eaten many different ways. They are made into foods like French fries and hash browns. They can also be mashed or baked.

Farmer Jesse, Farmer Terry's son, riding the potato planters

Potatoes are planted in the spring from a potato seedling. The seedling potato grows underground while the green, leafy plant grows above ground.

18

Potato roots where the potato grows

Potatoes need both parts to grow and thrive. If insects or cold weather damage the leafy plant, the potato underground could be injured or die.

The potato plant above ground

Potatoes can't be grown in the same ground year after year. They have to be rotated to different fields every year to ensure there are plenty of nutrients in the soil.

20

Freshly cut alfalfa

Farmer Terry <u>prefers</u> to plant potatoes in a field that previously had alfalfa because alfalfa leaves nutrients in the soil that is good food for potatoes.

Geese walking on ice near Malin, Oregon

Farmer Terry grows potatoes in Malin, Oregon. This is high desert, and the elevation, the height above sea level, is 4,048 feet. Because of the altitude, it gets so cold the birds walk on the ice instead of swimming in the water.

Potato field with Mt. Shasta in the background

Even though the potatoes stay roasty–toasty in the ground, the plant above ground will die if it gets too cold.

Potatoes being irrigated in June to prevent
freeze damage

It can be cold enough to damage
Farmer Terry's potatoes even in July. When it
is freezing, 32 degrees or colder, Farmer
Terry turns on the sprinklers to protect his
potato plants from the cold.

The water coming out of the sprinklers turns to ice when it hits the plants, which protects the potato plant from the cold like a big, warm coat.

Windrow digs up the potatoes and lays them
down for the bulker to pick up

Potatoes are harvested in October. In
an excellent year, Farmer Terry harvests
500 sacks of potatoes to the acre.

Each sack of potatoes contains 100 pounds of potatoes. That's 50,000 pounds of potatoes an acre, and in a 200-acre field that is 10,000,000 pounds of potatoes!

Potato bulker

To harvest the potatoes, Farmer Terry pulls a bulker with his tractor just like he did in college for other farmers.

Potatoes being put into the potato cellar

The potatoes move up a conveyor belt into a trailer hauled by a truck. The truck delivers them to the potato shed or <u>cellar</u>. A potato <u>cellar</u> is dark and cool, and it can be above or below ground.

Potato cellar

After the harvest is finished, the potatoes are moved from the potato <u>cellar</u> to the packing shed, where they are cleaned and <u>examined</u>. Only the <u>biggest</u> and best potatoes are kept.

Potatoes being washed for processing

Any potatoes that have <u>peculiar</u> shapes or have any damage are discarded. Only the highest quality potatoes are used.

Farmer Terry ships his potatoes to southern California. It is over 700 miles from where Farmer Terry lives to the processing plant. That is a long <u>distance.</u>

32

Farmer Terry's children, Farmer Jesse, Farmer Tara, Farmer Kari, and Farmer Karissa also raise potatoes, and Farmer Terry's granddaughter, Peyton, and grandson, Connor, help, too.

Farmer Terry's grandson, Connor

Connor's favorite way to eat potatoes is French fries. Farmer Terry loves potatoes fixed all kinds of ways, but he <u>prefers</u> them baked.

34

Peyton and Connor eating French fries

Potatoes are packed with all kinds of nutrients that are good for you, like calcium, potassium and vitamin C. Farmer Terry says, "However you eat them, they are delicious, so be sure to eat your spuds."

The End

Vocabulary Word List

Biggest
Cellar
Distance
Examined
Peculiar
Prefers
Surrounded

Author Biography

Kathy Coatney has worked as a freelance photojournalist for 35 years, starting in parenting magazines, then fly fishing, and finally specializing in agriculture. Her work can be seen in the California Farm Bureau magazine, *Ag Alert* and *West Coast Nut* magazine.

Visit her website at: www.KathyCoatney.com